The Book of Shares

Religion and Postmodernism
A series edited by Mark C. Taylor

Edmond Jabès

The Book of Shares

Translated by Rosmarie Waldrop

The University of Chicago Press   *Chicago and London*

EDMOND JABÈS was born in Cairo in 1912, where he lived until the expulsion of Jews during the Suez Crisis. He has lived in France since 1956.

ROSMARIE WALDROP, a poet and editor/publisher of Burning Deck Press, is also the English translator of Jabès's *The Book of Questions*.

The translator would once again like to thank the author and, especially, Arlette Jabès for their invaluable help and suggestions.

Originally published as *Le Livre du Partage*, © Éditions Gallimard, 1987.

The University of Chicago Press, Chicago 60637
The University of Chicago Press, Ltd., London
© *1989 by The University of Chicago*
All rights reserved. Published 1989
Printed in the United States of America
98 97 96 95 94 93 92 91 90 89   5 4 3 2 1

∞ The paper used in this publication meets the minimum requirements of the American National Standard for Information Sciences—Permanence of Paper for Printed Library Materials, ANSI Z39.48-1984.

Library of Congress Cataloging-in-Publication Data

Jabès, Edmond.
    [Livre du partage. English]
    The book of shares / Edmond Jabès : translated by Rosmarie Waldrop.
        p.   cm. — (Religion and postmodernism)
    Translation of : Le livre du partage.
    ISBN 0-226-38886-7 (alk. paper)
    I. Title. II. Series.
PQ2619.A112L5613   1989
848'.91407—dc20
                                      89-4928
                                       CIP

Contents

At an early age, I found myself facing the incomprehensible, the unthinkable, death.

Ever since, I have known nothing on this earth can be shared because we own nothing . . .

There is a word inside us stronger than all others—and more personal.

A word of solitude and certainty, so buried in its night that it is barely audible to itself.

A word of refusal, but also of absolute commitment, forging its bonds of silence in the unfathomable silence of the bond.

This word cannot be shared. Only sacrificed.

The Torment of the Book

Between one book and the next, there is the empty space of a missing book, linked with we do not know which of the two.

We shall call it *the book of torment*, appertaining to both.

There are books more favored than others.

They owe their privilege to chance, to various circumstances of which they took advantage in the course of composition.

They arouse envy.

Then there are books like this one, which have not been given any particular advantage except, perhaps, the distant support of a solitary author who, through all the hours of discouragement and silence, of expecting hardly anything more from his pen or the world, waited secretly, without admitting it to himself, for it to arrive.

"When did you begin to write?" an old man sitting at his desk was asked.

"The moment the book opened onto the book," he replied.

If God is the book His perfection can only be in language.

To introduce autobiography into a Jewish text, to rehabilitate the I— the particular that gives rise to the universal—to insist on the face and then proceed slowly to wipe out this insistence.

"One day we shall be able to read between the words, read the blank spaces through which we come to the words.

"On that day, God will have lost the book for good," he had written.

"What if the word lied not only to man, but to God also?

"Our idea of truth would be seriously shaken," he said.

God's truth is in silence.

To fall silent in turn, with the hope of dissolving into it.

But we become aware of it only through words.

And words, alas, drive us ever farther from our goal.

"We know," he said, "that no word can ever express us completely.

"Yet we are bound to choose one, to act as if it were the best, the *only one*.

"Here is the writer's drama.

"By himself deceived, betrayed.

"To know and deny it.

"To suffer and die of it."

The order of a book often means victory over oblivion.

How could we read a story studded with blank spaces?

It would quickly seem incomprehensible. We must appeal to recall, give in to memory.

Do not neglect any trace. Note them all with care.

There are no detours—a detour is a hole in memory. Fear of the unknown.

Lack. Lacuna.

A curve is but a straight line frightened by its own daring.

Reassuring image of the loop.

His crystal name, *Jew,*
Agleam in the firmament.
To crush the diamond, to spread
the tailings, fine residue, over the
ashes of our dead.
Dark splendor of beyond.

The last galleys brushed: page-proof.

Old characters assembled. Tomorrow, you will see a man's life revealed, with his consent. The title for this life still to be found. The void will come up with it.

A bird sails above our heads.

O mesh. Vestige of magnificent words that took wing.

In heaven, nothing to read.

We bury the dead with their book.

The Book

We shall never have been late for our life.
The book, an hourglass, always gives the right time.

Inheritance, I

We must cross all of night to reach morning.
Battle with every shadow, not by tackling, but taking them to ourselves.
Neatly dodging the difficulty.
Baffling their maneuvers.

Certainty may be a need for a man, but in itself, it is only a vacant reply to a penultimate question, with the ultimate left in suspense.
. . . vacant like a lot on which no building will ever rise because it would immediately tumble to ruins.

"My pen is honest," said a sage. "Words, alas, are less so."

"What is purity? Pure imposture.
"Lies are sometimes as limpid as truth," he said.
And added: "Because of this transparency we most of the time confuse them."

"Who could speak in the name of the ocean? Who could claim to be a mouthpiece of the infinite?
"A pebble speaks only to pebbles, but with words of the universe.
"Have I claimed to write from certainties?" said a sage.
"I write because I have none.
"A denial of our most trenchant assertions, the desert is a question to All and horizon of Nothing."

Never will a knife blade get the better of steel bars.

Never will sand disown sand.

Inheritance, II

"The divine call precedes God. The call of the word precedes the book," he said.

What a relief for the mind, truth; but once we have had a glimpse of it, what torment!

"There is no preferential place for the book," he had written, "but there might be a non-place made up of all the thinkable places."
This was answered:
"If nobody has ever found out where Moses was buried, is this not because there cannot be one single place for the Book?"

Truth cannot be divided.
It is shared from the beginning.
Remains to justify the shares.

"What you call *Truth*," he said, "is a truth in shreds.
"To each his own.
"Once ripped from the Whole, the miserable shred has no reality except for its misery.
"A truth of misery."

We are *for* truth. But what if this *for* were less addressed to truth than, for our comfort in thought and action, to ourselves, the presumed holders of this truth?
It would be better to say: We stay *by the side of* truth, as one stays close to what one believes in,

knowing full well that all belief is only self-recognition through what gives meaning to life.

A truth as justification of a life, in short.

"How do you see truth?"
"As truth sees me."

Shares of the universe, O book of perseverance and palpable poverty

Unprotected book—vulnerable, proffered, like a *bare face*.

God separated dark from light.

To his surprise, He saw day turn into night, and night, into morning.

Irresistible attraction of opposites.

A ring.

To read is perhaps to persevere in reading; to write—O fated words—is poverty perceived.

Our debt to the absolute can never be paid in full.

What if thought were only repentance of the unthought, a belated avowal of remorse?

As with a moment and the moment after, a word in a book can only be read through the word which follows. In reading a book we perhaps really begin innocently to read the future.

Candor of learning taking its first steps.

To preserve this purity.

Wisdom of knowing.

"To write means perhaps to speak for the first time," he said.

Who could ever write our displacement? It writes with us.

In my wandering, *I am its writing.*

*

"But let us go back to your phrase: empty envelope. It keeps bothering me.

"Empty envelope, right, like an envelope in which we forgot to enclose the message.

"That's what you mean, isn't it?

"Because there never is any message or, rather, because the message is really pure invention of the recipient. It is the message we expect and hope for, which we would like to send to ourselves and do, using our correspondent's hand.

"Giving and receiving here are one.

"What did I have to give or to receive? Nothing any more, having given all, received all. Questioning had left a void. This void was needed for a different, free, virgin exploration to see the day."

From the Desert to the Book
(Conversations with Marcel Cohen)

*

"What I have received as my inheritance," he said, "is the hope for a book.

"Poisoned legacy! With each of my works, a little more of this hope fades away."

And he added:

"Is the path we trace in writing nothing but the slow agony of a hope we vainly try to keep alive?"

Some claim that the first word was all the Hebrew people understood of the divine Book; others, that it was only the first letter.

Moses alone could reveal whole sentences, whole pages.

The Hebrew people read the book of Moses as we would read a book of which we only have extracts.

The entire book once transmitted, Moses fell silent.

In this silence, the Jews recognized their God.

Inheritance, III

Who is Jewish? Perhaps the person who, while never sure of it, by and by discovers his Jewishness in the probability.

Judaism is conjugated in the future.

To read in yourself—not only for yourself—the book you are carefully deciphering.
To read the erasures
under the writing.

"The essence of Judaism is constant recourse to citation.

"Ah, compared to the word Judaity, how luminous in its fullness the word *Judaicity*," said a sage.

Seal and Sedition

"And you shall write My Book by falsifying it, and this falsification shall be your torment and leave you no peace.

"My falsified book shall inspire another and so on till the end of time: for your line of descendants shall be long.

"O sons and grandsons of the sin of writing, lies shall be your breath, and truth your silence."

Thus God might have spoken to Moses.

And Moses might have replied: *"Why, O Lord, why condemn Your creatures to lying?"*

And God might have added:

"So that each of your books should be your truth and that, faced with Mine, this unworthy truth should crumble and fall into dust.

"There is My glory."

"Silence within yourself the dying Word which for millennia now has remained unspoken for the universe and only plagued saints and prophets.

"O irritable, perpetual night, night buried within the night of time of which you have, perhaps unawares, become the word of premonition," wrote a sage.

People of the Book
with Moses, after God,
as the letter
through which God became,
having ceased to be.
Interceding saints.

To ratify the Divine
absence. To write the text of
this absence as we read it.

"Every human word is an affront to the Word of God,
not because of rising up against it, but because it forces the
latter to repudiate it," he had written.

And farther down on the same page:

"What if this fierce will to replace or destroy each other
were their only way to exist?"

God is named at the most secret core of His absence.

"Perhaps our inability to live Godly is our liability to
die," he said.

Adam, or the Birth of Anxiety

Thus, along with lack,
anxiety was born.

A fallen apple—from the same branch that Eve plucked hers—continues to spoil at the foot of the felled tree.

Rotten fruit. Its name: ANXIETY.

Image of emptiness before emptiness.

Biting into the apple, did Eve know she was devouring her soul?

What if the book were only infinite memory of a word lacking?

Thus absence speaks to absence.

"My past pleads for me," he said. "But my future remains evasive about the assortment in its basket."

Imagine a day without a day behind it, a night without a previous night.

Imagine Nothing and something in the middle of Nothing.

What if you were told this tiny something was you?

And God created Adam.

He created him a man, depriving him of memory.

Man without childhood, without past.

(Without tears, without laughter or smiles.)

Man come out of Nothing, unable even to claim a portion of this Nothing.

Did God consider for a moment that with one stroke He deprived this man of what He would in the future grant all other creatures?

Adam, son of Nothing by the will of God, fruit of wanton benevolence,

fruit ripe before ripening, tree in full leaf before growing, world completed before emerging from nothing, *but only in the Mind of God.*

Man of strange thoughts on which, however, his life depends.

Man chained to the Void, chained to the absence of all absence.

The past reassures us. Man without such security, delivered to whom? to what?

Man without light or shadow, without origin or road, without place, unless part of that place outside time which is indifferent to man.

Things must feel this way. But no doubt even they have their thing-memory, recalling wood or steel, clay or marble. Recalling their slow progress toward the idea, the knowledge of the thing they were to embody.

O emptiness! Nothing to lean against, nothing to rest on, is this anxiety?

Time molds us. Without past there is no present, and the *I* cannot be imagined.

Orphaned in the fullest sense of the term, of father and mother, but also of himself—are we not engendered in that moment of carnal and spiritual experience?—what could seeing and hearing be for him? What could speaking or acting mean? What weight had a word, what reverberations in the future? What could it profit him? What contentment, what soothing could he expect from any gesture?

Discoveries, encounters, surprises, disappointments, wonder? Probably. But in relation to what other approaches, in reply to which inner question, lacking all comparison?

The key lies in the fertilized egg, the ovule, the fetus.

The mystery and the miracle.

The Book of Shares

Fertile forgetfulness. It pushes us to sound soul and spirit in the name of spirit and soul. It helps us clear the various paths of consciousness, to learn and unlearn, to take what is offered, whether by dawn or by night, *daily, in short, to create ourselves.*

I am not. All I have ever been is the man life has allowed me to be.

Thus I exist, molded by the best and the worst, by all I have loved or fled, acquired or lost, molded by seconds at the mercy of seconds as life drains away.

Eve came out of Adam's sleep, woke next to him by the will of God. She, too, a woman without having been a child, not having seen her body grow and develop, felt her mind open out, giving full rein to voluptuous sexual desires or fighting them.

They looked at each other without a word. What could they say? They could only observe, only study their difference.

Days of boredom, of uneasiness followed. Of anxiety, too.

They were God's playthings. Living together, yet unable to get anything from each other. Living, yet without landmarks of existence, not even a picture, a portrait which would bear out that they were real.

Only an unfamiliar body and a mind unable to think.

Enter the serpent. Enter into their ears the blandishing voice of the reptile, which was perhaps only the urgent voice of their anxiety.

Ah, this need to know, which on their part was not just curiosity, but the hope to be healed. For God had implanted suffering in them, the hurt of being. God had made a mistake. God had done wrong.

What if Eve's sin were really the sin of God which Eve, for love of Him, took on herself? Both a sin of love and the mad wish to save herself and save Adam?

Anxiety had encouraged the act, hastened the coming of their freedom.

Breaking God's commandment meant, for one and the other, finding their humanity.

Nature taking its revenge, the sin of the flesh will prove to be only the sin of procreation, of glorifying the seed.

Ephemeral eternity of what is born.

Eve and Adam cherished in advance, through the child-hood they never had, their fragile, future offspring. For God had already left them to their fate only to be in turn forsaken by them. Their freedom—O solitude and wound—issued undeniably from this double desertion.

But two questions remain.

Did God know, when He created man, that He could never make a man of him because he could only become one by himself?

Did Eve's weakness later seem a lesson to God, and to Adam, an essential test leading to their particular conscious-ness of existence, to the acceptance of life and death?

Gray Tint

Anxiety of white and black: Gray.

Words which had no time to turn black, so quick their passage—you might have called it stippled. But there remains this tint of gray they left on the paper, murky color, equivocal, familiar, so dear to our closed eyes.

. . . momentary thoughts, caught on the wing. Gray their shadow which, mingled with the dust, will never know it was once deepest night.

"When a written word turns suddenly from glistening black to gray, it is because the infinite of the page has paled it.
"O transparency!" he said.
And added, more to himself than to the others:
"Transparency, ah, there's the miracle."

Smoke. Smoke. The sky gray. Likewise earth and sea.
What keeps night from joining day is a death without precedent, which all the grayness in the world comes to augment.
Grief! Chasm!
Who among us will be able to describe what we know we have seen hidden in smoke? What calls out with its deep, haunting presence, yet stubbornly beats back our eyes?
Ashes. Ashes.
Ah, to love only what lives but for itself, so as not to be taken too quickly with what is dying.

"Confined—O paralyzing darkness—how could man attain God's solar words?
"You shall break the book of the seal.
"How could God, who is rising light, tarry on His way

for even a moment, where there is not so much as a glimmer, with our somber words?

"Only a few words separate man from God," wrote a sage.

Gray was the universe in its beginning.

"If you stare long enough at any being, thing, star, flower or pebble, you will end up seeing the emptiness inside it.

"Eye fatigue or peak vision, no matter.

"Emptiness has been sighted," he said.

Finite: all that is no more.
Infinite: all that is *more*.

Source Language   Target Language

To think of silence is in some way to noise it abroad.

Silence is no weakness of language.
It is, on the contrary, its strength.
It is the weakness of words not to know this.

"What is your own?"
"A breath. And it pledges me to death."

Rather than to sense, hold on to the silence which has formed the word.
You will learn more about it and about yourself, having both become pure listening.

Noise of the book: a page turned.
Silence of the book: a page read.
As if the transition from silence to silence could not be made without a groan.

Noise is deaf. Sometimes its infirmity makes it unbearable.
Silence is a universe of solitude. It requires a skilled and keen ear.
This is why often, wanting to make us hear at all costs what our ears have trouble perceiving, it is so painful.

Writing is an act of silence, allowing itself to be read in its entirety.

"It is because all of God's gestures are silent that they are written," taught a sage.

1

There are books which are "trumpeted about" and others which impose silence.

The former are tiny nothings steeped in loudness, the latter, tiny nothings that remain irreducible.

Writing means seeing as clearly by day as by night.
Eagle and owl.
Eagle in the morning light: the writer; owl in the dead of night: the word.
Fused into one and the same infinite attention.
Voice and breath define the space of the spoken word. External space. Vital.
That of the written word is the unlimited space of the book: night joined to day since its emergence from the dark.
O survival.

"Speaking," he said, "makes concessions to what can be communicated. Writing also, but tormented by the incommunicable."

He also said: "Thinking means ambling along with Thought.

"The thinker knows that the road is all he owns and all his future the unknown."

He had noted, "if I were asked which of all the mysteries will forever remain impenetrable I would not hesitate to answer: the *obvious*."

The Book of Shares

2

Siamese twins with separate heads: *thought and poetry.*

Everything is part of thought. So poetry might well be the expression of a double sensibility: of heart and mind. The word at its zenith.

Poetry thinks within poetry. Thought invites thinking all around. Chandelier hanging from a ceiling or light beam sweeping the sea, both are at the heart of all that is unforeseen.
Closed universe—deep enclave—of belief and disbelief. The only salvation is the exit.

Poetry, which is intuitive clarity, lightly clouds words in order to go with them to the threshold of day where the poem is written.
There is no mystery which cannot, sooner or later, be unraveled.

A poet thinks in poetry, in the exaltation procured by the poem; a thinker, in the discomfort which poetry has left in his mind.

As thinking by thinking, or love by love, poetry can only be saved by poetry.

3

"You want to leave. I know I cannot hold you. Neither with tears nor memories of laughter."

A woman's voice, voice of my native land, how many times has it collared forgetting?

The man who set out again had only an unfinished book for luggage.

O my love.

A sage said:
"For us, neither departure nor return.
"Only the long hard trek across the book."

4

To produce Nothingness.
To make it shine.

What if, behind the Nothing, a text were hidden?
A text of nothing.
All our books?

We breathe, we read.
Same rhythm.

Is it possible that written language is both *outside* and *inside* language, that it splits off from the common tongue a language apart, which it carries beyond language to a point where it is alone, facing the infinite, yet remaining still at the heart of that language whose possibilities it has exhausted?

You talk to people who talk to you. You write in a solitude where only the word joins you.

It is no doubt to this confrontation of two solitudes that the written word owes its particularity.

We have—as everybody knows—a mother tongue, the first language we learn to speak.

The Book of Shares

Armed with this commonplace, can we claim that there is a "mother page," a kind of writing we all share, page of our first stammerings?

But a child's first writings are exercises in penmanship, not attempts to discover our text of origin: *the text which engenders all texts to be written and which, though ever elusive, will not leave off haunting us.*

Writer's task: to read what is hidden.

Tonicity of the written.

We can say of a landsman: "He speaks the language just like you and me." Can we say: "He writes like you and me"?

No, because in writing, in the process of writing, something else happens, barely noticed, something mysterious and probably very ancient, which speech misjudges in its rush to assert itself.

Perhaps writing means, precisely, postponing this assertion?

We write between two renunciations.

Out of the words of his language, a writer forges new words, not neologisms, but words irrigated with his blood. He founds a second language which, to be sure, is rooted in the first with all its fibers, but which henceforth, being his own—O paradox—is nobody's. Because the writer's language wants to be only of the book, of the instant and duration of a liberated word.

Speech is audible only very near its subject, near what it is held to express directly. Writing, at much greater distances. The former speaks and has done, the latter keeps worrying what else should be added. The former encloses and discloses what it has seized, the latter encourages the statement to go beyond itself, only later to encircle its vertiginous unfolding.

We must not confuse clarity of language with the clarity of a text.

The former illumines on the surface, the latter within.
Fluid borders.

To get rid of a bad trump.

A writer's words have both more and less advantages than common words. This is their precision: this *more* or *less* being now what the writer adds (vision, daring approaches, dreams, phantasms), now what he takes away according to his own lack, his infinite emptiness which other words will try to reduce. So that writing always means hoping for salvation by a word still to come, *the writer being unable to express himself except in the future.*

Do not believe that an obscure kind of writing is obscuring one kind in favor of another, and hence passive.

A text lives and dies in the word, but of this death we know nothing, except that it is the issue of all speech.

"Engraved, the word erodes what it carves, be it marble or copper, only to be eroded in turn.

"Gorged with ink, it lets the page drink and then dies with it of thirst," said a sage.

And he added: "Sister of the book's faith in the book, O thirst, stubborn faith in the resurrection of water."

"Have you noticed those holes in the sand?" said a sage to his traveling companion. "They are the oldest known traces of words.

"And they are dug by the wind."

Springtime of the verb. *Vernation,* O leaf bud.
The order of the written is within the word.

The Book of Shares

The Dream

The apartment bell startles me out of my sleep.

I find it difficult to get up and go to the door.

A young man comes into my bedroom. "I'm the mail-man," he says and tries to hand me a letter.

Noticing that I have trouble lifting my arm to take it, he says: "I'll put it on the little oval table opposite your bed," and disappears.

Days, months, maybe years later, I find it again.

I open it and read at the top of the sheet:

B. D.

(I think of BOOK. DEATH. whose initials I have just been handed.)

And farther down:

"This is the end of all reading."

Three Legends

He gave his book to his Teacher who read it, rewrote it and gave it to his Teacher in turn.

The Teacher read it, rewrote it and, repeating his disciples' gesture, went to give it to his Teacher.

The Teacher read it, rewrote it and, likewise concerned about his Teacher's judgment, hastened to give it to him.

The Teacher read it carefully and, feeling that his four disciples had attacked his teaching, threw it into the fire.

*

To the rich man boasting of his fortune, the wise man said: "I pity your poverty."

To the poor man weeping for his misfortune, the wise man said: "I am happy for your riches."

As neither of the two understood his words, the wise man said to the rich man: "Your riches make you blind. For you, the morning is dense dark." And to the poor man: "Your eyes are so large through their tears that the world won't be long to take refuge there, to find a home in their total availability."

And he added: "It is God's poverty that His Creation can look with eyes so free and vacant as to embrace all the innumerable riches of heaven and earth rendered unto themselves."

"But I am hungry," said the poor man.

And the wise man wept.

*

When a disciple ventured that the divine Book was perhaps not as perfect as believed, his teacher replied:

"The trouble with God is that we cannot really know if He is altogether dead or altogether alive.

"In this 'altogether' lies His mystery."

And he added: "If He is dead we must accept His Book as unique and read it accordingly.

"But if he is alive we may consider His Book as a first work preparing the way for others, and our reading can't but be considerably modified by it."

*

"There are still some questions," said a commentator. "To start with:

"What if God were not the God of one single Book?

"Then we would have to search for the divine Word in other works.

"But who would dare risk that?"

*

"And what if the Word of God were intended especially to make us run this risk?"

"Ah, to hear, to see silence open out and fold back on itself. This is perhaps the divine message."

*

"Perhaps there is no divine book," said another commentator. "This would mean unconditional divine allegiance to a blank book."

*

Nothing is perfect. Everything to be perfected.
The future makes us and unmakes.

The Share of Goods

"What is your own? Almost nothing, and even this *almost* is too much.

"Too much, like a glass of water for someone who is not thirsty," he had written.

"One question we should never ask is: *What belongs to me?*

"A question I do ask myself: *What, my young friends, do you owe me?*" said a sage.

Adding immediately: "Nothing, no doubt. For what would my teaching be worth if nobody listened to it?

"My assets are more yours than mine."

"But what are these assets which we can never evaluate since they belong to us only to the degree that we relinquish them?" replied the disciples.

"Perhaps the weight of Nothing," said the sage.

"But what could Nothing weigh, if it is Nothing?" replied the disciples.

"What if its weight," said the sage then, "were the sum of knowledge we have accumulated over the centuries? A hoard of dust."

The sun is the star of poverty.

The question could have been my wealth if it were not itself so lacking.

We have one moment for the answer and an eternity for the question.

The sage is always one reading ahead of us.

All roads lead to death; only one, to the void.

To go forward, to forward what was before.
Fatal coupling.

Any end is perhaps only the hasty union of male fire and female fire.
Disgrace of enduring.
One fire one flame.

Let us also side with the spacing, the between-the-lines, of a text: both a promise and a breaking of ties.

From reinforced thread to threadbare: the course of a life.

He had once noted: "To lead the past to its fulfilment does not mean to impose an end to it, but to attribute a function to the future and so, perhaps, give it meaning."

Hier, "yesterday," could have rhymed with *lier,* "to bind," but is pronounced differently.
Can we ever, the way we bind words and sounds together or from within, tie down what takes pains to slip away?
Wager of ties.

The readable is perhaps only the unreadable smashed to pieces, a grandiose spectacle of havoc.

Fragments of fragments.

As the passage from writing to the written does not leave a trace, it is always primal, not originating *in,* but *against,* its origin. Undisclosable beginning.

Death is a spider spinning its web; the word, a fly caught on the wing.
O posthumous birth of the book.

Once written, the *I* is nothing but writing which has drained the I.
Ratification.

Some ashes have been mine for a moment: the remains of a burned book strewn to the wind.

Dust has no power.

Twine: harmony.

Kinship between two languages. *Skin*grafts.

A leaf in the wind, a grain of sand retrieved by the desert.
You read this retrieval. You read the desert's victory over the grain of sand, then, unexpected turn—reverse, reverse—the victory of the grain of sand over the desert.
Every book is first of all a book of history.

Sap rising, surging life, O truth.

To refurbish time, the builder of centuries.
To whitewash the walls of the Temple.

Small flame. Small flame at the heart of sleep. Its soft light favors the blooming of dreams. Nebulous spiral, O nocturnal version of history hidden from the sun.

Costly unreality.

Cutting. The diamond submits.

From its place in the dark, the candle moves, drawn up into the wavering light of the flame.
If it seems to melt down, this is an optical illusion.
In reality, death irrevocably pulls it beyond its decreasing light.

Dazzling emptiness. Supreme burn.
Two universes for one sun.
O night, peaceful rest, space saved from silence dark with closed lids.

We shall have lived the death of a life that infiltrated ours, the life of the book.
A word for a fraction of a moment.
Thus we learn to live and die of the joint readability and unreadability of one and the same existence.
To the rhythm of our pulse.

If you knew how fragile our houses are, how fragile yourself, you would tremble.
Weakness where strength is measured by the number of exploits. Resistance of all weakness. Surrender of all strength.
Man and book are equally vulnerable. Man in his body and mind, the book through the words which undermine it.

For the *You* to be really *You,* the *I* must first really be *I.*
"Who am I?" is echoed by "Who are you?" But this question is bound to dissolve in the question.

To be able, one day, to close my life as one shuts a book, convinced that there is still a treasure hidden within.

Any possession frustrates exactly at the point where it encourages us.

Paper. Paper.

We perish of what has made us be, much more than of what we are.

None of our acknowledged property is exclusively our own. However, the pleasure it gives may well be.

"We knew we owned very little," wrote a sage. "But we had never considered that this little is still not our own."

We can dispossess only ourselves.

Writing under the writing. Under-writing. Not as in a guarantee, but as in something understood, as the chord subtends the arc. O distant aim. Words of another memory.

To die before the word, to abandon it to an orphan death.

We shall have written only what writing itself prompted.

Listening is quiet. Did we suspect that it is a page of writing snitched from the eye?

White. White.

To read what recedes.

Drought. Famine.

Every word is first of all the echo of a lost word.

Death can act fully where it is sure to find what it looks for, but not where we, alas, have nothing left to offer.

The right to die, under these conditions, is perhaps only the legitimate right to deny eternity the ultimate gift of ourselves, a chance to die voluntarily, with something still our own.

"My life is worn thin with friction," he said, "an old rusty cable which chafes, but will not give, as long as the ship of years counts me among its gear."

The Book of Shares

And he added: "Perhaps this is the image of a life, this constant wear and tear on an unprotected rope: marline or gammoning."

Nothing can chain the light.

We don't spend our death. Life is frittered away, dying.

"What is said is sometimes reinforced, amplified by *repetition*.
"For each flagging voice its *repeater*, its amplifier.
"The word hangs by a hair and moves on a wire," he had noted.

To acquiesce in death's proposals.
Weakness of soul.
To die without getting dire.
Flower turning fruit.

Every beginning appropriates the outset. It is not already there, but a refusal of the *already*.
Sharper's shell game.

Demarcate our property. Well, we need to know how far it extends.

Night tells its tale.
Dark legend.
Words shrouded in gloom.
Dearth. Dearth.
White, the finale.

In the process of writing, words lose interest in the written, as travelers charmed by the road forget their destination.
No allegiance to a text here, only submission to the process of writing.

Do not let the words sour. Their longevity is like that of wine.

Sourness of the skinflint.

Accept me as I am not. You will force me to disown myself.

By this stratagem I can perhaps learn from you who I could have been?

You want to think everything, but your mind cannot do it.

Between wish and ability, O infinite, O emptiness of the unthought.

Sun.

Lone eye.

He said: "Picture thought as a plant, a tree, a flower, a fruit, even a blade of grass.

"And the unthought as the sky, the blue sky, the sky of day and of night.

"The unknown makes us thirsty.

"Water, water or we die."

You have opted for security, tranquility: for the *answer*.

I have chosen insecurity and worry: the *question*.

I mark time at the edge of life whereas you have already reached death's shore.

To die on the threshold.

Man created God by bestowing on Him the purest attributes. He killed Him by withdrawing them, one by one.

Cut the wings of your allegations. You will see them crawl in the mud like worms.

Who writes for me? What is writing itself in my name, this very moment? How can I distinguish what I write from

what a quicker hand—but how did it eliminate mine?—
tries to pass as my offspring?

There is one who is silent within me—with me—when I
fall silent.

There is one who speaks within me—with me—when I
express myself.

Is it the same man?

"We are part," he said, "of Nothingness.

"Any dividing of goods is a dividing of the self."

What does God's "Get thee out" to Abram mean but:
"Let your progeny take your wandering presence as a luminous pledge of My all-powerful Absence"?

Could I be Jewish to the point of identifying with the
venerated propagator of this terrible commandment?

God's silence is the abyss of the word.

Poised infinite.

The Unlimited   The Limit

The limit is neutral because it is already part of the unlimited.

Speech makes us giddy. Books, never.
There is an audible silence: writing.

The Stakes

The hand knows its limits, the page does not even conceive of them.

Around you, the invisible. But you see with your attention.
Eyes supplanted by sight.
Ah to seize, to seize the infinite.

A sound—uttered by whom?—and then nothing.
A word—written by whom?—and then a blank.
Listen to the nothing. Read the blank.

To hang just on a wing-beat:
Misplaced faith.
Porous, casting no shadow, neither heaven nor earth could hold back thought.

We tend to judge others on the strength of a word given.
Writing, too, has its *givens*: its references, landmarks, alignments.
Its frankness and its cunning.
Its convicting evidence.

A mortgage: language.

What if, for any language, God were the gauge of silence?
The inexpressible.

God cannot be named. God's name is: the unnamable.
Celestial silence.

Is a name an obstacle?

To have no name. Is "no-name," being a lack of a name, also the *no* in the unpronounceable divine Name? The first step into the invisible, the unutterable?

A victory of fore-telling over the un-told?

Did you expect, with the help of a chalkline, to set perfectly straight limits for thought?

Fluctuating, the line between life and death.

Limits rise in tiers all the way to the infinite, like, on their own scale, an adolescent's clumsy sentences in his copybook.

Do not oppose silence and noise.
They operate in relentless relay.

He said roses were half silence and half scent. This made them so beautiful.

Will we ever know if it is their beauty that is fragrant or their fragrance that conveys their beauty?

Watch our for infatuation. It has an aftertaste of lies.
A bitter aftertaste of treachery.

Do not come out of your reserve. Insist on it.

Reserve even now the right to be alone with yourself at the supreme moment when you first dip one foot in the void, as you once dipped it for the first time in the sea.

Respond only to the time you have left. You will meet deadlines sooner, arrive more quickly at your last word.

My limits are my liberty.

The infinite is infinite closure.

"In order to have freedom we must have had constraint, for there is no freedom except where it can be exercised.

The Book of Shares

"We have given the name 'Freedom' to what is only the means we use to be free," he said.

God knows no freedom.
Nothing resists Him.

Did I already know that opening and closing my eyes, lying down, moving, thinking, dreaming, talking, being silent, writing and reading are all gestures and manifestations of subversion? Waking upsets the order of sleep, thinking hounds the void to get the better of it, speech in unfolding breaks the silence, and reading challenges every sentence written.

Did I know further that there are degrees of subversion, that we are truly subversive in our relation with others only when we do not at all try for it, when, in an atmosphere of non-suspicion fostered by our natural behavior, nobody notices?

At every moment, life rises up against death; thinking, against the unthought; the book being written, against the written book.

To live, to think, to write engage us in an oblique search for inner balance in the face of

Three "blurbs" or quiet prayers to push back the limits of the book
. . . with a subterranean—as opposed to sovereign—voice, so as to be heard by the dead buried with their book.

A book of prayers is perhaps only the favorite prayers from the book.
We have made its choices our own.

Every thought is a prayer of the mind; every word, a prayer of a text; every death, a prayer of eternity.
To pray: to clear away stones.

Do not try to overtake the word. It has long left you behind.

"In a text," he said, "everything goes by so fast that, unable to gauge its

subversive acts, a balance we finally achieve by allowing them to clash inside us.

We are the battleground of these conflicts. We manage to contain them locally and space them out in time. This we call: living in harmony with ourselves.

speed, we think it is all glued to the page."

What if subversion first of all subverted itself?
Disappointment and grudge of dialogues.

(*Le petit livre de la subversion hors de soupçon* [The Little Book of Subversion Above Suspicion], 1982)

One more book—not an extra one, but one *more,* as there can be one more degree in heat or in our relation to writing and the infinite.

The road I have taken was laid out by my books, and each in turn kindly set up milestones.

They were sacrificed to the unlimited.

She asked the man who sat waiting for her without really waiting if he knew the name she would have liked to bear in order to exist.

As he remained silent she slipped away and disappeared forever.

The reason all dialogue fails is that we are unable to reveal ourselves to anybody as we really are. Strangers facing strangers.

"Man," he said, "prays with words of flesh and soul; a stone, with words of dust and sky; grass, with words of blades and dew; the sun, with words of light and heat; the sea, with words of salt and waves; the flame, with words of burns and ashes."

"And flesh and soul and dust and grass and dew and light and salt and waves and darkness and heat and ashes?"

"Grass, dew, light, salt and waves, darkness and fire, dust and ashes are in every prayer," he said.

A carver of niellos will never carve words.

A book for death against the book of a life.

But dialogue thrives precisely where, across the silence which is the base of the book, two powerless utterances desperately confront each other in search of their truth.

(Le livre du dialogue, 1984
[The Book of Dialogue, 1987])

At this point of the road, no doubt worried about precision and objectivity—but can we be objective?—I had to rethink my relation to Judaism and to writing.

To a certain kind of Judaism—have I stressed this enough?—which is mediated through the book and recognizes itself in it.

These pages could have taken the form of a journal. They are part of my life.

All reflection is speculative. We question first of all what we have invented.

And who knows if invention is not itself a truth or, in any case, our only means of attaining truth?

Nothing is given. Everything is to be taken—to be taken in.

. . . once this point of contention is cleared up, the road will immediately be illuminated.

(Le Parcours [The Route], 1985)

Prolongations

... the distance from subversion to dialogue, a crack where life wells up, where death infiltrates.
A faultline.

A flaw: straw in the iron, amazement in the diamond, tongue in the glass.
Impure, our death.

How can I acknowledge you? How listen to you?
Will barrenness in the end win out over spirit?
Distance covered. A crevasse—brook, river, stream—a trickle of water, tireless murmur, keeps the world awake.
What do I expect? Is our greatest expectation not the hardest to define, the least necessary, hence the unforeseen?

Minor mutations. Voice break.
Could inventing simply be venting a secret?

Light, light, O night, to grind the stars.

There are no ties except of love.

*

Bundles of colored strings, knots before the letter, words before the word.
Were the illiterate ancient tribes aware that every word is a challenge to Creation?
Their book of strings offered the reader only despair at being unable to escape loneliness.

"Leave, take your distance, get away from me," said a sage to his dumbfounded disciple. "Don't you see that I am bound to eternity whose insensitivity is incommensurable?

"Soon I too will have a heart of stone."

The distance covered. The future already no longer there.

"There are works," he said, "which have never seen the light, but whose words feed and spread nostalgia.

"Out of these melancholy words we intuitively fashion a book of regrets."

"The visible," he had once noted, "is not the negation of the invisible, but its perverse expression."

"The call of the abyss."

Like the world, like life, the book has its season and its off-season.

Subversion is perhaps only a *rotation of crops*.

Sterile soil, arable soil, or
the Nothing of a dream of existence.

To find a balance within the imbalance where our energies plunge us.

In the way that illness is cured with illness, we can foil subversion by using it.

Thus, lighter than water, the ship embraces the sinuous wave which had often tried to sink it.

"Man," he said, "has slogged away at subverting the Book of God, while God, on His side, quite serenely subverted that of man."

What if the unpronounceable name of God were only a shunned name with four flammable consonants?

. . . destroyed because irrefutable?

The Book of Shares

Watchman of the book run aground, of the book covered by night.
All reading exhausted.
Useless watch. Watch over Nothing.
Desert. Desert.

Limits imitate limits. All space is sham.

Subversion has neither beginning nor end. It upsets alliances and reverses situations.
A trap.

TRANSPARENCY! Who could still doubt there are miracles?
Divine, hyaline act.
Pact of alliance.
No bounds for the unknown
nor frontiers for the infinite.
Horizon. Horizon. Horizon.

Indivisible invisible.
To see. Primal
choice.

He said that everything became so limpid for God that His eyes now go through the universe without seeing it.
Nothing now separates God from God.

> ("*And me, my love,*" she said, "*do you want me so absent that you don't even notice how your eyes pierce me like an arrow and each time draw a little blood from my body?*
> "*I only exist for the pain, and it excludes you.*")

She was reduced to the scent of woman, to man's desire for his love. Ineffable joy.

There is, on the one side, the innocent reality of dream and, on the other, hard reality into which the dream empties.

But between the two?

What if every stone's vow of purity were only a haunting memory of crystals, an obsession with what is beyond reach?

And if that which is beyond reach is all we have ever hoped to seize through the things we could approach, brush against, touch?

And if of all our shipwrecked words only one, the toughest, had survived, lucidity of the Void which rivets us?

Do not be surprised that you have sometimes gone bleeding along the road. The universe is glass. Your path is strewn with shards which the light kindles into a hundred borrowed colors.

Transparency is light's fortune.

But we cannot leave out the night. Night denies all differentiation.

Never, ah never, will you have been so alone.

Liaison

The horizon exaggerates the nearness of the horizon.

Custom

You think you have gained a book. You have lost it forever.

Trust your body to bear the hardships of exile; trust your mind to oust oblivion.

Virgin thought, a path through the forest, cleared by the knife.

Convincing break-through.

"The riches you have amassed over the years are no more than those you have squandered during the same time.

"You go from the fullness of poverty to poverty stripped of its own," he said.

To inhale the human, the scent of the soul.

"Do not ask me who I am," said a sage. "I do not even understand the question. Hence I have long stopped asking it.

"Ask me instead where I am going. My surprise will tell you that I have never worried about it."

Forgive my writings. They have the excuse of despair.

"God's point of view," he said, "is a *point*. Hebrew made it a vowel so that, now that all writing has become readable, God's point of view could be read in every word."

. . . at this point of convergence and conflict.
A star.

You cut to the quick of the days. The future wears the modest blush of dawn.

Impatient newborn, who could wash you clean of your mother's wound whose crushing memory will kindle remorse till the day you die?

At no moment are we safe from ourselves.

Can we think what we see, touch, hear for the first time?
Can we think astonishment, wonder, disgust?
Yesterday has been thought. Tomorrow is unthinkable, although expected . . .

Could it be that the thinker is a creation of thought?

Then thinking would mean being shaped by our thought, being the live model to which it sacrifices us: *our own frightful double.*

From the unformed and unthought, thinking draws its new form.

Hence the unformed is perhaps the vast night through which all forms must struggle, and thinking, the radiant break of day.

The life of an idea is ours insofar as the idea belongs to us. But how can we imagine this? On the other hand, how can we not?

The idea blossoms and wilts within the idea.

We do not lose our ideas in the course of the days: they let go of us.

A thought reaches its completion only in the thought which refutes it.

The Book of Shares

To convince, not to constrain.

With supporting arguments, every page of writing tries to persuade the following one that it must continue.

A book is a series of mutual concessions. But to what can we trace the persuasive power of the word?

Perhaps to the intensity of its silence.

Silence is the bond.

II

> Only the Void is entitled to vouch for the Void.

Seductive unreality. Despotic.

Will we, some day, let go of our cumbersome dreams?

O night! Reality is perhaps only the object of a fresh— startled?—lease on consciousness.

Comforting thickness.

Who would push absurdity to the point of trying to mold what is not susceptible to external pressure? Our breast is not wide enough, nor our arms sufficiently long to embrace the universe.

Space gets in the way. Distance is the enemy of our daring. Do not venture too far into the unknown. Do not hoist yourself too high into the sky. You had better not dredge too long the bottom of the sea. You could choke to death.

The laws which govern the book have no power over the voice: they are even under its sway, viscerally.

The voice of the book is older than its laws.

He compared eternity to a lamp which nobody has lit and therefore nobody will come to extinguish.

Light to closed lids, dark to eyes that open.

A scream. Suddenly the night is nothing but uncontrollable fear. Infinite trembling of stars and the flare-up of ancient terror.

To die, ah to take and lose heart in dying.

Voluptuous slide from almost to nothing.
Naked unknown.
Every mystery disturbs by its wantonness.

If I had to find an image for the secret, I would opt for an unveiled woman, because the veils, once dropped, strip her of all image.
Thus the face made transparent is replaced by an infinite absence of face. O mocking emptiness, indifferent to our beseeching hands, careless of the unforeseeable consequences of what could never, will never ever take place.

Secret. Secluded woods.

The first book is a peak; the last, roots.
Now to become a seed of absence.

III

"Answer any question with a question of the book," said a sage.

If you happen to speak of my relation to Judaism, do not ever call it just Judaism, but *this particular* Judaism.
Between your night and mine, there is the stubborn infinite of an unconditional night.

"All that for a 'Perhaps'?"

The Talmud

All that for an "Almost"?

. . . almost a glimmer, perhaps of morning?

I was writing at my desk. In spite of the late hour I was not at all sleepy. Still, I must have closed my eyes once or twice. Everything around me seemed no longer quite real.

Outside, night was testing its horizons, adjusting its frontiers.

Suddenly, three men came out of the half-light. Without any effort, so great was my surprise, they seized a stack of my pages.

One said: "These pages are mine." The other two visitors: "And those are ours. We wrote *almost* all of them."

I objected: "*Almost,* you say? Then *perhaps* I am the author of some of them? The ink on my fingers would seem to prove it."

They continued: "These pages are ours by right. We have come a long way to retrieve them. After we have examined them we will give you back the rejects."

"So many days and nights," I thought when they had gone, "so many sacrifices and tears, and all that for an *almost,* all that for a *perhaps?*"

I found myself alone again, clasping to my chest a sheaf of crumpled pages, all blank, all strangely blank . . .

IV

There is no joyful death, but there is a joy which fills death with bliss.

Between letter and word, a fragile bridge connects the reality of Nothing with the unreality of All.

What if this bridge were an arch dreamed across the abyss?

Eternity would be more vulnerable than time.

Time is protected by man. Eternity has no defense.

We recognize one another, not by the abundance of our riches, but by the merit of our spending.

Thinking passes where the idea has already passed by.

No matter how violent, a gust of wind in the desert can only whirl up a bit of sand.

"If I saw you I would know where you come from. My eyes have taken in so many centuries," said a sage.

What if time were man's experience of consciousness?

Then eternity—this deep and infinite sleep—would be the time of the unconscious, would exist as time erased from the conscious mind. Atemporal time. Desert time.

But whoever invokes supreme authority turns his back on the grain of sand.

Time can perhaps be conceived as a reduction of eternity: a "diseternalized" eternity.

Here, the desert is omnipresent.

Dormant eternity.
Truth with closed lids.
Life drains away. A moment.
Euphoria of lies.

To answer for . . . To answer to . . .
To live. To live.

For me, the detour through Judaism was maybe the shortest cut from the particular to the universal and from the universal to the particular.

Even the broadest highway was begun by joining one stone to another.

"You must realize," he said, " that in spite of its prestige the Royal Road, when you look closely, is quite an ordinary road of low extraction."

God knows what you know, but you do not always know what God knows.

And yet, you are the one who thinks.

"Master of the answer, God tolerates only the question. And yet it gives him nothing but trouble," a sage had written.

To learn what God, maybe out of indifference, does not trouble to know.

Then there would be a part of universal knowledge to which only man had access. One more confirmation of our solitude—and His.

And what if our anxious questioning no longer interested God?

Oblivion. Celestial oblivion.

Could the taboo on representation be above all a taboo on ideas?

Ideas: loaded dice in the hands of Satan.

To strike the mind in its main functions.

God is saved by the void.

"Do not depend on ideas, those blind arrows.

"Learn to handle the bow: thinking," he said.

Experienced fisherman. Patient.

What if thinking were a bait, and ideas, the fish?

Remains to define the sea.

What if God who invents and absents Himself were caught in this dilemma: to condemn or encourage His creatures in their attempt to catch a glimpse of the divine?

In God's despair lies, perhaps, infinite hope for man.

Messenger of the soul, O word so inward that it disconcerts the ear, trembling to make itself not just heard, but sensed and felt entirely.

O shivering, voluptuous caress. There is an intoxication in silence, as there is pleasure in water touching water.

Silky skin.

"You think of the world as a sandworm would think of the ocean. God thinks of creation as an eagle flying over the desert might think of a pebble he noticed in the sand," he said.

And added: "To think of the void as worms think of the corpse, their stinking universe."

V

                . . . this heaviness which posits lightness.

Is being language? Is language recognition of being?

Being holds language (which cannot encompass it) in check, but language likewise checks being (which cannot master it).

Then being owes its possibility to be to language, and language owes to the meditation of being its possibility to exist.

Bond of nothing and nothing.

Of Void and Void.

Of empty and empty.

Hyphen of ashes.

"What if the past (which has done waiting), the present (which is waiting) and the future (which has broken off the wait) all three together formed a frail skiff which, no longer parting time, were to push its own duration into the very heart of the moment?" he said.

And added: "Past and future are not, for all that, the now present in writing, but the now before and after *what is gradually being written*.

"Unsuspected dimension of the text.

"Do the four horizons not fight over a pebble?

"No word for eternity.

"Books, the writing of time.

"Scrawls."

Silence precedes us. It knows we will catch up.

What if time were only the instinct of duration? Then the moment would but consecrate time's flair. Sap, O movement of dream through flared stems which in the flower joins with the boundless desire of flowers: inrush of the infinite.

Then thinking would perhaps be only *foreboding*, and the thinker a kind of magician, a divinely human diviner with exceptionally keen senses?

"Thinking," he had written, "is the fruit of a particular sensitivity to the surrounding world, an unerring intuition of man's final development."

Sometimes what's easy turns hard.

Disloyal difficulty.

"If of the ten braids which by and large bind us together a single one remains undisclosed, it can cause irreparable breach," he said.

Truth comes to us naked. We dress her in veils.

Each time we put another over her shoulders we think we have taken a step forward, as if going toward Truth meant progressive obscuring.

Being dazzled does not agree with man.

The proof: it blinds us.

In what calculation did nature indulge to so disgrace the desert?

Truth, sister to the grain of sand, perhaps alone knows.

"The desert is not death. Neither is it life. *It is a test of life*, a test of strength that life sets up against militant death, "as it used to be a test of freedom and love," he had noted.

To dress life
in armor.
To unrig death.
Utopia.

The *I* is not the stake, but the game.
Mirror. Mirror.

Life contemplates death and sees itself as it will be.

Silence: the sleep of birds.

"For origin," he said, "knowledge has the *no* of the ig-norance it grew out of, a denial, likewise, of all origin."
And he added: "The unsaid is not necessarily unthought. But the unthought is always unsaid."

Creation is thought in the future tense, in the wake of a still more distant future.

Purveyor of prows, O thought, brave thought.

Jewish people, contemporaries of a past and future to which you have given your voice,
death, for you, has never been dead; life never once been taken from you.
Thanks to your faithful memory you endure.

Faces

. . . this world has a face: ours.

Turn your face to me.
Is the universe really this small?

A face grows old with its name already aged.

A stranger. After so much wandering. After
building and rebuilding how many times?
What, ah tell me, you who know me, what
have I kept for myself?

Asoluteness of Nothing.

We had our kings.
But those kings are dead.
We had our princes.
But the princes perished.
We had our wise men.
But, being wise, they turned the page of their
life.
We were a people.
But this people scattered.
We are a book
at the heart of the fire.

With the flames which, one evening, licked our
books, we shall paint a living face on every fire-
screen.

As long as it has not burned us, the fire is no fire.

It is but a mock image of fire.

The Void is bound to the Void.
Sovereign cord.

A breath, and you exist. Little by little, you struggle out of anonymity without an inkling that you are in fact going toward it.

Your face reflects your age. If you grow old it means you grow. The age of your face is fixed by death.

Your life can be seen in your features, your death guessed in your wrinkles.

Beautiful what breathes, hideous what breathes its last.

The hour will come when your face turns from your past forever.

It will face itself without mercy.

Any reserve of the present is a secret surplus of past.

Welcoming a face we celebrate the world.
Rejecting it, we condemn the world.

There is no peak that mankind cannot scale.
Death knows it well, guarding the highest.

It takes much love to survive love which, in its paroxysm, may without inconsistency turn into hate: hate of the other from mad love of self.

What if wisdom were only the mind's tenderness toward the heart?

Anticipate. Recapitulate. Your life is both the past moment and the moment which passes it.

Do not rush. Haste would be fatal. Do not shrink back either.

Light, air, voice, your life's vibrations.

Your soul: life.

Like sadness or joy, like tiredness or rest, time has many faces.

Fascinated, eternity borrows each in turn.

Out of the thin fog of absence, out of the distance where it was hovering, a face approaches. Trust your eyes.

There are no dream portraits.

Since writing means above all trying to stay in the text, I have discovered a strange kinship between writers and the aficionados of an outmoded card game called *reversi,* where the winner is the one who has taken the least cards.

Writers have no past. Neither do books.

The mind grows green again, O dream.

Dream, but so modest, so quiet: dream of a grain of rice.

So weighed down with centuries, the book you unearth.

Each of your sentences makes it younger. O treachery, is it enough to erase the obelus in the margins to make it *your* book?

Thinking clarifies nothing but thinking.

The dead have their shrouds. Death has its darkness.

The porous soul, its infinitely frail protective coat: a leaf.

II

A face of which only wrinkles are left. A face with its daily life shattered, its eternity blurred.

Unclaimed. Having tumbled beyond the horizon and taking time with it.

Here, the past is rendered to the past. Over there, the future, studded with the unknown.

O torment. The infinite is not a high sea turned gold by the sun, nor a night attended by lofty stars.

The infinite lies ahead. What still resists is no doubt what has duration on its side.

But is duration not constantly threatened by itself? The menace does not come from the sacrificed moment.

What is destroyed inspires relief or regret, but never causes fright. A stubborn perseverance, on the other hand, is daunting in its insolence.

Being flesh and bone as well as airy thoughts, we are bound for dissolution. What cannot die has an edge of strangeness which both distresses and fascinates us.

To aspire to be. To be nothing any more but this aspiration, yet feign to be unaware. Our natural death is doubled by another which falls indifferently on all Creation and of which we are both terrorized victim and lucid witness.

Eternity does not attack the fleeting moment, but the glorious one which digs in.

Fear of dying and of surviving, twofold fear which mocks our impotence and gives the book the shivers.

I write, not to steady this shiver, but to prolong it, as if all that mattered were to feed this pleasure-tinged fear without which I would not exist.

God is not death, as He has never been life: He is the unfathomable ambiguity of both; for what is dying but being born unto death, what is living but dying into life?

God is saved by His facelessness. He has created the incomparable face out of what may once have been His. He is supreme creation, but also sovereign destruction, hence without likeness and, like the void, unmatched.

The desire to create frees us from the Creation. As this desire is moreover a desire for itself, our firm resolve to produce always wins out. We create against Creation with the freedom it grants us.

The Book of Shares

What if God were only the divine passion of the universe for the universe, the concrete proof of such perennial passion?

What if absence experienced presence as a brief awareness of its own reality, intimations of possible resignation, sudden need for a face?

Wanderings within God's incommensurable absence.

Would a fly dare compete with an eagle?

Spread out, the pointed wings of the sky graze both horizons with every beat. The sun is its heart. Folding its wings, the sky robs the light of space. They go down together. Fatal flaw in the infinite.

Night is a chasm, the grave of a dead bird mourned by the stars. O infinite grief. And in the distance everywhere, drawn by the fire, moist eyes from the far side of life, sorrowful, awesome.

We have only one history, which we repeat imperturbably: of the planetary light which, at the appointed time, dazzled the universe.

Our history is in our retina. Every image returns our face. Death briefly held in check, O face of the world become ours.

A wall rises in your path. Oblivion hardened by oblivion. Future of a forgotten past. But, with years of erosion, the wall will show cracks.

Widen, if you can, these fissures, the welcome retrieval of the past. We enter the future with limited luggage, not allowed to take everything—says who? Our wick burned down, naked, finally, we go out among the shadows.

There is a curse on our features. Pariah face.

And why not a rose aglow in its misery, a face of prophecy or, better yet, stubborn grass with its bitter hope out of time's reach?

Sterile plant, windfall of the Void.

Party time. Let us celebrate the marriage of deprivation and radiance.

Royalty is internal.

Thirst holds more water than the ocean.

Low tide, O tired face. Do you recognize it? Piteous face of a life.

Though you did not stare at it, but at a fixed point, dim, and yet so clear.

Face of the book. *Your face reflected in words.*

Every family its portrait album. Nations their history books, countries their legends, people their memories, the little they remember.

A face is not where it is matched, but where it casts off the ballast of its appearance, its allegiance.

This face unknown to my eyes, but so familiar to my soul, I can reconstitute in its smallest details. It was once pure space of mind, a crossroads of adventurous thoughts until, in the fullness of want, it became the face of the abyss.

I remember a day when, looking at the fading beauty of a sage's lined face as he bent over his book, I felt with near-certainty that eternity had chosen to mark its hidden comings and goings in the quick of his flesh.

Eternity works in secret. It is betrayed only by the absurd setting of due dates.

Wrinkles which are not creases of skin, but perhaps lines of words in the last stage of being erased, when nothing can be read any more.

Thought is often late for itself. The book never lags behind the book.

Innocence. Innocence.

As a child, I could with a few sticks or matches reconstruct the landscape I had dreamed the night before.

I managed to people it with characters with whom I maintained close and mysterious relations.

Their faces never left me. Yet I cannot say that they intrigued me.

They were present like death and life. Identifiable through what continued without them and what had only been.

Who can say how a trembling as faint as that of a rose losing its first petal could survive the book?

The book says nothing but this shiver.

At the Mercy of the Threshold

A shadow is transparent only for shadows.

The acquired: precarious support.

What belongs to me is what holds good among what is no longer mine.
A cork at sea.

Wisdom is not in knowing but in having known.

Like a bumblebee against a window pane, the moment bumbles against the infinite and dies of its self-inflicted wounds.

"We are vile blasphemers," wrote a sage. "We cynically interpolate into the Book of God ever larger fragments of our own works.
"Additions (our only wealth) versus God's (only) goods."

I think of the unknown child whose birth will coincide with the moment of my death: one single moment for life and for nothingness.
And I tell myself that we shall both inhabit it forever, myself assuring the continuity of what has ceased to be, the child drawing his life from it.

To form a link between life and death, O lucidity! To be this knot strengthened by the instant.
What if death brusquely untied it?

To form a link between what, by dint of not being, is without reserve and what, by dint of wholly wanting to be, is no more.

O sleep. O waking.

Vague border.

A duopoly, the association of writer and book.

To sell Nothingness for almost nothing.

Indivisibility of God, all symbols once abolished, at the heart of the Name.

The safest, best defended stronghold of silence. Place without place or, rather, place within the non-place of the book.

Seedbed. Tomorrow we sow.

"At night, sleep follows the blind movement of our eyes from sky to earth, from root to mountain top, alert for the moment when fatigue takes hold in order to reign, finally, over our soul and body at its mercy.

"But strangely, it is sleep which, at daybreak, gives us back our strength," he had written.

A man asleep is as weak as the night.

"Our power, no matter how extensive, is never more than accessory, hence negligible compared to God's.

"And yet God's power would cease to rule the world the moment it lost the support of ours," a sage was wont to say to his disciples.

"There was so much left to say to the man who had resolved on silence that one morning he opened his veins in order to dissuade with this spectacular gesture any word from still calling on him.

"Do not imitate him. It would be absurd, because useless.

"Words are fickle. Somebody else would immediately appropriate them," he said.

And added: "Don't be too hard on words. They sometimes have trouble reaching us where we are never sure we are."

To hold our own against silence.

"A dream was my possession for one day, poverty for all my days," said a sage.

To write means perhaps only to adjust, to get used, by and by, to the night of the word.

Do not lose sight of the beginning. Only through other interposed beginnings can you approach it.

Not: "He died of . . . ," but "he *probably* died, of . . ."

To introduce the notion of the problematic into the text. Opening.

To muddy the water with a bit of ash.
Allow the unforeseen, the chance event.
Dethrone the system.
Get the seal of approval from the possible.
Make wide, wide the margins.
The brand: death's imprint.
Due.

We see only the future. Yet it is the present which kills us.

Eyes gone blank from scanning space. Nothing but endless, endless sky. Blue, so blue before giving in to night.

Nothingness can also flaunt its colors.

He watched the sea die into the sea and said to himself that life hangs on a glance.

Let God lower His eyes, and we are no more.

At Auschwitz, the eyes of all the lined-up prisoners hung on the guard's right thumb. To the left, death; to the right, life, for the time being.

But newcomers to the camp would only see the incomprehensible, regular back and forth of an official's finger.

What if silence were a word which by signifying nothing still signals this nothing to disappear?

A flaw in the structure of language—fissure or feint of the word?

And if it were only the lifetime of a breath?

Readability, audibility always at stake.

Words stubbornly refuse to recognize anything but words.

As the river narrows, the water is weaned from space and accordingly increases its pressure on the banks.

But is it the spring or the ground that is responsible?

Red river bottom.

The sea has no confidante but the sea and no witness but the sky.

There is only one infinite.

Could it be that the improbable is not so much a denial of the probable as its impulsive or—who can tell?—instinctive resignation? The quiet joy of having nothing more to expect from the future?

Receding horizon of what has been.

The Book Read

When ashes turn into a posthumous book, the words are reborn from their first sound.

Audible post-mortem. Have we made it legible?

You have stopped listening. For you, the universe has been.
You have rejoined the beginning where, divine, words will engender silence.

"Silent eye. Hand released from the hubbub around.
"We only read, only write the book of silence," he said.

A page of sky. A page of sand.
A book of ashes.
Between, both separating and joining them, the hollow line of a life without issue.

He thought he had buried his book.
He had only buried his hands.

Shortly before his death, a sage decided to leave each of his disciples a portion of his most precious possession.
But how to do this when it was a book?
He gathered them around and said: "Every book is ashes gathered from the single book which our burned words periodically come to enlarge.

"There is no reading of the book. We only read its being consumed in the ever revived fire of creation.

"A flame, our pen."

And he shared out evenly among them a handful of grey dust.

"A blind sage, a dumb sage, and a sage gone deaf would add up to three invalid sages if they were not really all the same person: blind facing God, dumb facing the Text, and deaf to the lure of our frivolous words," he said.

We should consider childhood as the first unveiling of our origin, adolescence as the second, old age as the last.

Life lays bare our beginning.

Starry night. Hidden treasure.

Light. Light.

We have used a ray of sun as our road, but it was only a bright line death had drawn across our life.

We are born and die bathed in light.

The same light, no doubt.

"God is everywhere. Here and elsewhere.

"After having been all the letters of the alphabet, He is all the accents lacking from the Book," he had written.

And added: "The divine Book embraces all the unfinished books of man.

"Hence, thinking we read God, we only read ourselves.

"Are we not right to claim, on the strength of this significant discovery, that God is within us and that the soul is one of the immaculate pages of His Book?"

"Death," said a sage, "is perhaps only the book of a life whose pages have been erased."

The hour to abandon his book had come.

He took it in his hands, not to reread it, but with a long, gentle caress fingered page after page, line after line in order to soothe and close forever the thousand questioning eyes fixed on him—words of which, at the edge of the abyss, only a stare was left.

Immediately, all the stars in the sky went out. He felt paralyzed facing for the first time utter night, the absolute negative of the unknowable.

It is not nothingness which roots us to the spot, but the sight of the Void.

For the first time he felt weightless. Unburdened to an extreme degree. Disintegrated.

O ashes of contentious immortality within God's radiant immortality in ashes.

Dust. Dust. God turns away from Himself.

Could He accept His defeat calmly?

Lasting history of dust. History of man and the universe.

Have we not paid dearly for our shared dream of eternity?

And did God know that immortality was only the other side of death?

"When God wanted to destroy the earth, a great fire burst from the ground, sweeping Him into the conflagration."

"But God is not dead.

"When God wanted to blot out the sea, a giant wave broke from the others and carried Him off in its fury.

"But God is not dead.

"When man opened the book and shattered it—O grief—a ravaged landscape lay before his eyes.

"And he drowned in his tears.

"But man still exists.

"Here is the miracle," he said.

"Every act of thinking, of love, of life entails a detour through death.

"Here is the source.

"Fruitful oblivion," he also said.

To open the shipwreck unto the void.

Parting of the waters! Our limits are within us.

To assure the relay. From book to book.

Come. Take your property in which I have buried mine.
   The book in its infinitude is perhaps only a partial dividing of the void where the world is written in the uncertain words of fate.

   Global, the divine view of Creation, yet minute detail is its security.

   "One single word is enough to designate the universe," he said, "but how many words do we need to put it ajar?"

The Example

Providential gap.
Between fire and fire,
where the swallow flies,
where passage means sharing.

"Is King Solomon's verdict the verdict of God?" a man of the law asked a sage.

"God inspired it," was the answer.

"And the mother's sublime sacrifice which shames the inhuman verdict of her God and her king?"

"God inspired it likewise."

"That reassures me," said the man of the law. "For then God is as green as we are in matters of sharing.

"And as unprepared, faced by what is just."

Justice is locked into its narrow tract. The judge sometimes dies for lack of air.

To open the splay till it is wide open.

Burned Pages

1

Cut with impunity to the quick of the blaze.
Shares are apportioned with a blade of flame.

There is no limit but has been deeply felt—
a trickle of blood, and already a border to cross.

The book of shares is the book of limits.
On one side, fleeting lamplight, on the other, the
dark unknown.

Sharing has perhaps no other aim than to lift a
corner of the heavy, dark curtain of our solitude.

"Justice shares the remorse of the just," he had writ-
ten in his worn notebook.

We cannot escape ourselves. We keep testing this
reality.

There will always be more sand in the desert than
the wind can whirl up, and more ashes in our hands
than they can hold.

"To think of sharing," said a sage, "means calling morality
and law into question. It also means challenging the notions of
happiness and misery. It means, finally, taking action against
humanity, against life and death.

"Everything must be shared yet nothing can be: man's fate as
well as that of the world. This intrinsic difficulty is perhaps the
basis of reciprocal gifts."

And he added: "And yet, to exist means increasingly to open
up to sharing. It means sharing our life with life, our joy with
joy, our sorrow with sorrow, our death with death, in short, our
moment with the moment."

Could it be that in itself sharing is nothing but arbitrary
seizure?

In being born I grab life, in dying I ransack death, unawares I loot the beyond.

Actions can only be judged in their fullness. Likewise feelings. Our behavior is our own.

We act as if we had all the rights in the world. We move as if nobody else wanted to budge.

Infinitely diverse the motivation of our leanings or revulsions. Motives are personal.

We burden others with the full weight of our reason, sensibility, complexity, or indifference. We must be accepted as we are. This is how we establish relations with others. This is how time and eternity work, to which we are subject.

Can we, under these conditions, think of calmly parceling out some particular possession: gold, money, love, convictions, ideals, ideas? And what value can we bestow on a gift which by definition excludes equitable shares? It will overwhelm one and disappoint another, its value altogether subjective.

Our riches are nothing unless endorsed by all.

Here is the difficulty. It does not result from the nature of property, but from its destination despite choice. For just distribution depends on everybody having the same capacity to enjoy the property received. It implies the same idea of, the same interest in it.

But who can estimate the true price of what he owns? To own nothing still means owning this nothing. Nothing, like all, cannot be divided, being always all or nothing in the infinite of all and of nothing, and nobody will ever succeed in taking its measure.

Could sharing be impossible because we are all different?

For two people to share a love, to live the same life, surely means they each live to the full their portion of love and life. Across the other, we are only concerned with ourselves. This is the condition of sharing. Hence it is basically an illusion. The other gives us back to ourselves and vice versa.

To share a bed, a meal, never means more than securing a place in the bed or a portion of the meal. But the place agreed on, the portion of food will needs vary according to how big your body or appetite. No matter if it is a bed, a meal, a life: we never go halves.

Exchanging is not sharing, for unlike the latter it implies complicity.

In an exchange, we give less or more than we take in. It could not be otherwise.

Books illustrate this perfectly:

We cannot share a book, if only because it elicits such diverse approaches.

It sends us back to one single book: the book created by our reading.

Having read it, we have shared nothing, but kept everything for ourselves or else given it all without return.

After God's crushing example.

"How can we read a page already burned in a burning book unless by appealing to the memory of fire?" said a sage.

He also said: "The trace left by a book is perhaps only a lingering smell of burned moments.

"The time it takes for a small heap of ashes to be consumed entirely is a variable of its endurance."

He said further: "A flame remembers only flames.

"Thus a pact with the book is a pact signed with fire.

"The name is the first to go."

In the end, he said: "We can only use words we know. Hence any book we write is a book we have already read."

And added: "Writing means perhaps desperately destroying our very work, obsessed by the book we shall never write."

O thought cleansed in fire.
Limpid eternity. Are we aware of it?

It is enough to come near the sky to find ourselves
in the shoes of an anonymous intruder.

Death is the master of shares.

2

These few burned sheets were originally pages of a private let-
ter. Long after, I came to understand that the fire had returned
them to me.

A letter which probably never reached the man (or woman) it
was addressed to. For, strange as it may seem, the envelope was
intact, still glued shut.

With what kind of troubling intention had it been written?

So flatly, no, so shamelessly insistent that only urgency could
justify it.

To convert in order to destroy.

The envelope is still in my hands. I thought for a moment I
could (alas, without success) decipher the name which is still on
the tip of my tongue since I could never pronounce it. But per-
haps it was that of the unidentified young woman who came one
morning to ask me for it, for the name that had been hers and
which she had mysteriously forgotten.

What if this name were also the one I have vainly claimed for
myself and which slyly undermines the name I bear?

And what if this missive were the same an unknown mailman
one day put on my table and of which I could only decipher two
letters at the top: B. D.?

A flame will never obliterate a riddle.

"With my books I feed the fire while it feeds me my
death," said a sage.

"The future is based on a wasteful selection, and
we cannot make head or tail of it," this sage also said.
"For nobody could prolong what is lost or blot out
what continues."

Truce: a dream.

"Listen. Do not assume that everything is de-
stroyed for good.

"*Does a flame not piously retain certain phrases from our consumed books and, in burning, recite them one by one to the flames?*

"*You need only prick up your ears to hear them again distinctly.*

"*O singsong of nostalgic conflagrations,*" he had written.

"*How can we divide the name of God with its four unvoiced consonants?*" he asked.

"*We shall only have apportioned silence.*"

And added:

"*Moreover, if we cannot share everything, what remains forever beyond sharing? What will never have been ours at the very heart of our possessions?*

"*And if we shared only the vital desire to share, our only means to escape our solitude, the void?*"

Dawn

Make allowance for fire where writing spreads.

Fire attacks the book at its vulnerable extremities.

Ah, one more moment to save from the flames the few words chance has chosen to close a life.

Did not some sage say: "Having opened your book throw it into the fire so that every word be the familiar prey of the flame which reads it?"

. . . I saw him leave. From the back, I could identify him by his walk.

Was it really the man with whom I had gone everywhere? And why did I let him go on alone this time?

I felt tired beyond words. To give up going, give up wandering.

I sat down on a nearby milestone.

Steps which seemed close made me suddenly jump up.

Already. Already time again for the road.

The man, my guide, my companion, my daring and relentless double, stood before me.

He handed me a book which I opened rather hastily. However, as I tried to decipher it, the text vanished.

Behind us, abandoned embers of a fabulous conflagration, the last glowing logs of my soul, showed signs of dying down.

Ah, write, write to keep alive the fire of creation. Raise words from the peaceful night where they lay buried, words still astonished at their resurrection. But, O fatal folly, is it only to surrender them to the impatient flames of the void which will devour and reveal them to death, because suffering is their lot?

Dawn, the book's vast desire.

Did we know, O destiny, that the dazzling morning of writing was only a mirage in an ashen desert, a mirage from beyond, where fire is at its zenith?

"The book of shares," he said, "is perhaps only the book of a hope shared by words whose dawn and dusk—O clear keys—were waking and death."

From the heat of their first blaze to its battered dying down, our glowing words shall have set bounds to the abyss.